Citrus Stains

Ivy Lemon Haycox

BookLeaf Publishing

India | USA | UK

Presentation by *BookLeaf Publishing*

Web: www.bookleafpub.com

E-mail: info@bookleafpub.com

ISBN: 9789360949006

First edition 2024

This book is dedicated to myself, to my growth, to my journey.

ACKNOWLEDGEMENT

Special thanks to my support system, to my ride or die. I love you, Lilly. Please know that I do not ever want to know life without you.

Additional thanks to all the supportive women (and Ian) who proofread my poetry and did not recoil in horror at my raw emotion.

Honorable mention to my ex husband for proof reading every single one of these poems and protesting that he just doesn't understand poetry.

PREFACE

Last year, my good friend Shelly gifted me with a little program through which I published my first poetry collection. This year, the dame went and did the same thing. If you know Shelly and happen to like this second one, or the first ("Inky Lemon"), go ahead and send her like, chocolates or something. I know she is particularly fond of Vienna sausages.

"Interacting with you is like taking sandpaper to my heart"

Holy little flower of mine
Pet yourself with this rake darling
Pretty pretty thing
I'm busy in the garden
I love you so so so

Spinning dancer of my eye
Hold your own hand
Moon of my world
Pin it to the table with my nail gun
I want to kiss you forever

Goddess of strength
Haven't you learned not to need
Golden cherub
I have to finish this round
But I swear it's us it's us

Sparking sparkling diamond girl
Your teeth are getting sharper
Little cherry chariot
Let me grab my file

I would go the world for you

Statuesque picturesque queen
I apologize darling, for leaving
You feathered flighty thing
I promise it was good for you
I promise I needed you too

"You try your ass off"

You tried
Buttered toast
And carcinogens
You tried

Where have you been all my life
Where were you when the towers fell
But fighting to survive all alone
You tried

I planted forks in your arms
And centipedes across your teeth
And asked you to smile
And you tried

You tried, plastic heartbreak
You tried to feel
You tried to tell me
I was your cage, your downfall

And I heard you trying
I drove miles when you tried
Paved your heart for my travels
Made an adventure of your trying

I exalted your tries
I painted them into galleries
Poured them into casts
And displayed sculptures of your try

I swear
You tried
You swear

An Honest Conversation

5

Sometimes I picture
Walking across some very long hall
Toward you
And the closer I get
The greater your grimace
The longer the train of my dress
My hair messes
My breath quickens
And from under your coat
At the last second
You reveal a dagger
Carved with my name
And already dripping
And just before I reach you
I am back at the opposite end
Of that great and infinite hall
To walk toward you all over again
But I never escaped
I am already wounded
And my dress is stained red

"You are correct, no end in sight."

Penelope,

I fought for you.
I loved you.
I owned you.
It was all I had longed for
These many years.

Penelope I died for you.
I dug my own grave
And pulled my own trigger
I cleaned my own blood
From your carpeted bedroom.

You are correct,
Penelope, flower and sunshine
Waves and sand and newborn turtles
You were right all along
You knew everything

No end in sight.

He/Him

Not all men
Are animals

God I wish my husband were

I wish he were teeth and claws
And bloodthirst

But my husband is a docile puppy
A cooing sleepy baby
Rocking to sleep
In the cocoon of his own privilege
Mental and experiential
Fluffy, white, cottony privilege

Lulling him to sleep
All day and all night
He has the snore of a man
Without concern
Without belief in his own fallacy

He has the walk, the lilt
Of a mind without weight
The soles of his feet are made of aluminum
Whereas mine as made of lead and steel

I wear knives and mesh as fashion
I have spikes on my collarbones
Titanium in my knuckles
I have an exit plan for every building
A takedown strategy for everyone I meet

He has to reject promotions
Because privileges fall on him like rain

And my rain is cigarette smoke
Is scars I measure in inches and hours
My rain is acid, is cum
Falling on my face like ash and snow

Cat Claws Down A Curtain

It splits with ease
Each time,
Like cat claws down a curtain
The knife separates
My left side from my right
But nothing comes out

No blood, guts, gore
Santitized, clean, rippled pages
Fluttering open
With a shhhhhhh
Down the center
Whispering while I sleep

If I were to wake
I'd cry without blinking

I Am Poetry

I am poetry

I am so fucking tired of being poetry.

I am clipped phrases and feelings
Pictures and monologues
Tiny but overwhelming
Moments

But I want to have
Recurring characters
With arcs and backgrounds
With hometowns

I want to be
The cardigan I perpetually wore when I was
sixteen
The ring my uncle once made me
The video games I grew up playing with my
friends

Double oh seven
Ivy pendant
Foreign exchange temporary cousins

But I am feeling
I am desire
I am the embodiment of matricide
Of violent protest
I am a fist in the air

And god I am so tired.

Open

Open wide

Open wide
Open wide
Open wide

Open wide

Hangnails
Screwdrivers
Shark fins
Open wide

Penetrate the reality you live in
Open wide

Be the only thing you know for certain
Open wide

Let the blood soak the linens
Let the men have their privilege
Let the skies become livid
Open up

The Thing Driving

You don't know it.

You haven't named it
Like I have
You don't play its circle rhythm
On your record player
Or ask it what it wants

To eat today

You have never once noticed its dancing
Its puppetry over you

But it fills your chest
On the daily
It makes your breakfast
Eggs and coffee
It lifts your fucking legs
And sets your feet on the floor

And would you like to know
Why you've never noticed?

Because it's never left you.

You've never howled in terror
At the loss of it
At the absolute horror
Of the void when it leaves you.

Scorpion

15

Swallowing my pride
Is feeding my pride
And discussing my feelings
Is only feeding my neglect

So I'm a scorpion
I wear flowers and pearls
Lace and velvet
But I'm really a scorpion

Stinger protruding from under my dress
Barbed wire girl

"Your presence is the very last thing I need."

Your hips are my heaven, your
Presence is my oasis
Is this true joy?
The needle in my chest says it's something
Very akin to death
Last time I took a breath, that
Thing filled my chest
I need your heat
Need your fingers to trigger my death

It Helps

17

It helps
It helps no one
It helps no one to call
It helps no one to call my partner
It helps no one to call my partner a bitch
It helps no one to call my partner a bitch or a
cunt
It helps no one to call my partner a bitch
It helps no one to call my partner
It helps no one to call
It helps no one
It helps

"They are out there acting as your own PR team."

I am not an island
Though I have many islands

In each place I have known
I have spaces filled with love for me

Little nooks and crannies
Of safety all over the world

And you call them
My PR team

"It is horrifying being in a relationship with you."

When we were all little
We married our dolls
And each other on playgrounds

When I was little
Sex sounded horrible
And I wanted nothing to do with it

But I wanted what we all wanted
Or what we were taught to want
A boy who would be a man

Who would love us and tell us so
And twirl us around in the sunlight
As our circle skirts fluttered in the wind

And then each time I watched
A boy become a man
I was horrified

"Aren't you miserable?"

I'm falling through the forest canopy
And never landing
Impaled and gasping
Gripped by terror
Grasping back at the branches
As they shoot past
Getting handfuls of leaves
Of anything but you

"Why do you feel this relationship is worth saving?"

I didn't give up until I had nothing left to fight
for.
I didn't give up until I had nothing left to fight
for.
I didn't give up until I had nothing left to fight
for.
I didn't give up until I had nothing left to fight
for.
I didn't give up until I had nothing left to fight
for.
I didn't give up until I had nothing left to fight
for.
I didn't give up until I had nothing left to fight
for.
I didn't give up until I had nothing left to fight
for.
I didn't give up until I had nothing left to fight
for.
I didn't give up until I had nothing left to fight
for.
I didn't give up until I had nothing left to fight
for.
I didn't give up until I had nothing left to fight
for.

I didn't give up until I had nothing left to fight
for.
I didn't give up until I had nothing left to fight
for.
I didn't give up until I had nothing left to fight
for.
I didn't give up until I had nothing left to fight
for.
I didn't give up until I had nothing left to fight
for.
I didn't give up until I had nothing left to fight
for.
I didn't give up until I had nothing left to fight
for.
I didn't give up until I had nothing left to fight
for.
I didn't give up until I had nothing left to fight
for.
I didn't give up until I had nothing left to fight
for.
I didn't give up until I had nothing left to fight
for.
I didn't give up until I had nothing left to fight
for.
I didn't give up until I had nothing left to fight
for.
I didn't give up until I had nothing left to fight
for.

I didn't give up until I had nothing left to fight
for.
I didn't give up until I had nothing left to fight
for.
I didn't give up until I had nothing left to fight
for.
I didn't give up until I had nothing left to fight
for.
I didn't give up until I had nothing left to fight
for.
I didn't give up until I had nothing left to fight
for.
I didn't give up until I had nothing left to fight
for.
I didn't give up until I had nothing left to fight
for.
I didn't give up until I had nothing left to fight
for.
I didn't give up until I had nothing left to fight
for.
I didn't give up until I had nothing left to fight
for.
I didn't give up until I had nothing left to fight
for.
I didn't give up until I had nothing left to fight
for.
I didn't give up until I had nothing left to fight
for.

I didn't give up until I had nothing left to fight for.
I didn't give up until I had nothing left to fight for.
I didn't give up until I had nothing left to fight for.
I didn't give up until I had nothing left to fight for.

"Maybe this is just you, and I have to live with that"

I was never much of an artist
But here I was holding my greatest work
My most impressive creation

Each detail, especially the eyes
I had truly outdone myself
What a fucking masterpiece

I thought to hang you
To recreate you
One for every room

I had been approached to sell
And I was horrified at the thought
I could never part with you

But then
My specimen, my grand prize
You just had to go and speak

"I'd appreciate it if you turned on your location sharing"

I'm not watching
I'm just looking

Just peeling your clothes off with my teeth
Just begging for your last name

I'm not following you
Just going the same way

I'm not touching you
I'm not here for you

Just drinking your air like my third beer
Digging at you until you disappear

I'm not your nightmare
Just sitting right here

"I promise to not ever misquote you"

In sickness
And in health
I hope you learn to love yourself

I hope you take your hands in yours
And dream to be the perfect lover
I hope you are made for each other

Time after time
To the moon and back
You must, I pray, I beg of you

Be the tired sleepy arms you lay in each night
Be the fog you drive through to get home
Be the only airport in town

Don't be mine, be yours.

"Prove it then."

I spent last night on the bathroom floor
And I spent this morning on the roof
I tried to crawl into a cupboard
When they started asking for proof

When the world was younger
So inevitably was I
There lived a spider in my head
Spinning, weaving threats no one had ever said

The spider grew with each new web
And lays now outside of my head
She is gravid with secrets known not to me
And heaves with stories in her abdomen

The weight of my proof
Is too heavy for webs
It is thick and stinks to high heaven
And so my quotes pierce her through and
through

She bleeds silken blood
Each thick thread a thought I had

Untethered

It comes swiftly and violent
From under the covers
Flapping its wings, pecking my ears
Can't help but discover
The highways, the slants of the roads
I don't know which way's east
Until mountains utter…

This way, this way, this way, this way
And my full mouth blubbers
I have seen what happens that way
What's only felt by birds
Even worse, that way is Texas
Where no girl should ever return

And I am a dive bar bralette
A dripping wet concern